FAIRACRES PUBL

WITH ONE HEART AND MIND

PRAYERS OUT OF STILLNESS

ANTHONY KEMP

SLG Press

© 2023 SLG Press
First Edition 2023

Fairacres Publications 197

Print ISBN 978-0-7283-0342-3
Fairacres Publications Series ISSN 0307-1405

Designed and typeset in Bembo by Julia Craig-McFeely

Cover image: Hayling Island by Daniel Kemp

SLG Press
Convent of the Incarnation
Fairacres • Oxford
www.slgpress.co.uk

Printed by
Grosvenor Group Ltd, Loughton, Essex

Contents

Special Prayers

Foreword

During the lockdowns of 2020 and 2021 we all had to learn how to pray in isolation from one another and without the familiar comforts of the worship and company of the Church. During this time Tony Kemp started composing prayers to share with those he served, and he carried on after the lockdown finished. These prayers come from the overflow of a life lived in communion with God. They are offered here as streams of thanksgiving, lament, intercession and hopeful entreaty to the God who continues to find us and serve us, even in isolation. May they aid you in your prayers and bring you close to Jesus.

Stephen Cottrell
Archbishop of York

Preface

Hayling Island, the author's home, has been known as a sacred island since well before Roman times. One of the largest and most prestigious Roman temples was established at the northern end of Hayling Island around 60 AD replacing much earlier shrines dating back to the Iron Age. Today the Island has three Anglican Churches, two dating back to the eleventh century built by the monks of Jumièges Abbey from Normandy. St Peter's, which was originally built as a chapel of rest at Northney is marginally older than St Mary's Priory Church in South Hayling. The third, more modern Anglican Church, St Andrew's, is situated at Eastoke.

In recent years a group of five people regularly met for silent prayer in St Mary's Church on Hayling Island every Wednesday at midday. When the Covid lockdown occurred in March 2020 it was decided to continue the practice of silent prayer, separately, in the privacy of members' own homes. The prayers in this book were written each week to offer focus, if required, for their solitary prayer.

During the following months the group expanded through word of mouth to become a community of about thirty participants, drawing in a handful of others from much further afield. This practice continued through-out the lockdown and restrictions on gathering together, until the following September when the churches began to reopen for communal worship. By that time the collection of prayers was quite large.

These prayers seek to support and sustain people in prayer throughout the changing seasons of the liturgical year, with sections related to the liturgial calendar, celebrating the lives of the saints, and addressing various day-to-day concerns. Their purpose is to support those seeking a deeper, more devotional prayer life. They are intended to induce the wonder and mystery of intimacy with God encountered in all things, visible and invisible. They are written to encourage a sense of intimacy with God, seeking a sense of awe and wonder of God's presence during prayer time. They are designed to encourage a slower, more reflective approach to intercessory prayer. They are particularly appropriate for use in private prayer, on quiet days and retreats, but can be used in public worship settings. They are theologically orthodox and sometimes reflect an Ignatian influence, which I hope will suggest further imaginative reflection and delight in God's heavenly kingdom.

A key aspect of the collection is the section for the lives of the saints, which includes a small number of holy days. This section dwells on interior spirituality in order to inspire new personal spiritual insights. These prayers aim to bring the saints to life colourfully, encouraging readers to connect with their own inner spirituality and to reflect on their intuitive and emotional responses. By these means the author attempts to articulate warmth and intimacy with God in Christ Jesus. This is the essence of affective prayer of the kind advocated here.

These prayers are rooted in the tranquility of the coastline around the author's home, and the sea with its changing ebb and flow.

WITH ONE HEART AND MIND

The Seasons
of the Church Year

Advent

Come, Lord Jesus, come down and break into our lives
with the sound of good news;
Come in the splendour of Your eternal light to shine on
us who walk in deep darkness;
Render us receptive to Your call to repentance seeking
spiritual pathways to new life.
May the great light of Christ shine into our hearts and
minds that yearn for Your closeness.

Make us a godly people, guard our souls from evil and
nurture us at the sacramental altar;
With the saints in light may we shine forth with Your
love and compassion in the world;
Until that final day when we stand, ready to see You face
to face at the judgement throne.
May Your peace, love and justice reign here on earth to
Your glory as it does in heaven.   Amen.

Christmas Night

O silent, awesome night when God stooped down from
  heaven to meet us in humility;
O holy night of expectation, anticipated in wonder by
  Your children across the world;
God made man, lying in straw and vulnerable;
  the holy mystery of theological complexity.
Attune our ears to hear the singing of the heavenly
  angels: "Glory to God in the highest!"

O God, give us eyes to seek the light of the natal star, to
  wend our way to Bethlehem;
To seek the Christ child, God incarnate, and to fall to
  our knees in homage before our King.
O Love that comes down at Christmas, fill our hearts
  with compassion for the homeless;
We seek to worship You with the shepherds, the sheep
  and the oxen, in concert with
The angels, archangels, the celestial choirs and the
  whole of creation.

Cold and hungry and unloved, asleep on our street
  corners under bedding of rubbish.
Give us grace and courage to draw near, to come close
  and to see. For there we may find
The Christ Child, God in loveless poverty, who has
  established His home among us.
Maranatha. Come, Lord Jesus. Amen.

Christmas Day

Joy has come to the world! Our God has stooped down
   from heaven to dwell with us.
At the dawning of the day, the singing of the angels is
   replaced by the lowing of the cattle;
The long-awaited Saviour of the world; the defenceless
   child born in poverty, sleeping in straw.
Praise God for this wondrous event of Divine Love;
   the world never to be the same again.

May the love and peace of Christ fill our hearts as we
   pay homage alongside the shepherds;
Touched by the loving devotion of
   the Blessed Virgin Mary and Joseph.
May we be ever mindful of the homelessness of the
   Holy Child of Bethlehem and
Empower us to give hospitality to the homeless; to be
   ever mindful of the Holy Child obscured by the
   extravagance of Christmas.
In the name of Jesus, the Christ Child, we pray.   Amen.

Epiphany

Open our eyes, O Lord, to perceive the brightness of the
dawn that is breaking upon us;
Transport us out of our deep darkness to journey
onwards towards Your marvellous light.
Be our true light, illuminating our pathway to come
into Your presence with joyful hearts;
To be filled with the radiance of the break of day and
ready to proclaim Your greatness.

We arrive with all that we possess, to present ourselves
before You in wonder and praise;
The Child of Mary, the mystery of the Word made flesh,
full of grace and truth.
Lord, as we struggle on our journey in search for You in
the remoteness of our hearts;
Search us out and know us; come and make Your
dwelling place within the depths of our beings.
To You, O God, be all thanks and praise for evermore
and evermore. Amen.

Candlemas   The Presentation in the Temple

O God, we venerate saintly Simeon who recognized
   Your Son as the Saviour of the world;
Cherishing the Christ Child cradled in his arms:
   the light that enlightens the nations.
May we, likewise, embrace the Holy Child, the true
   radiant light that shines into our hearts;
Dispelling the dark shadows that remain, lingering on in
   our wayward tendencies.
Lord, our Father, help us to grasp the fulness of Your
   love that came down at Christmas;
May our candles of commemoration light our pathway
   on our journey towards the Lenten fast;
Turning to face a pilgrimage of self-examination and
   self-denial to perceive the Pascal mystery;
To grow in devotion and holiness in the company of all
   the Saints who have gone before us.
In the name of Jesus, we pray.   Amen.

Ash Wednesday

Praise be to You, O Lord, that by Your Holy Cross You
have redeemed the world.
Give us the grace to own in true penitence the ashen
cross signed upon our foreheads;
The cross of baptism, of absolution, of blessing and
peace, of the rites of our final journey.
May we know our mortality, seeing that all is dust, yet all
ending in the joy of harvest.

As we enter this time of self-denial and solemnity we
hold in our hearts all those who suffer an enforced
wilderness of deprivation, hunger, homelessness,
and depression.
Lord, help us to find the balance between our inward
stance and outward concern for others;
To strive for the coming of Your kingdom of justice and
equality here on earth as in heaven.   Amen.

Lent

Lord Jesus Christ, Son of the living God who endured
    the trials of the wilderness;
Help us by Your grace to withstand the temptations that
    appeal to our weaknesses.
Give us strength to turn away from the darkness of evil
    and fill us with Your glorious light;
Give us true and contrite hearts and a deep desire to
    turn away from sin;
Remind us that You created us from the dust of the
    earth and formed us in Your image.

When we find ourselves in a desolate, arid and loveless
    place where our well has run dry;
Send Your holy angels to protect us from the snares of
    the enemy and all evil.
In these Lenten days help us to remain alongside You
    and to listen to Your voice;
Inspire us and confirm our desire to live in humility and
    grow in discipleship;
In the name of Jesus our Lord and Saviour we offer
    these prayers. Amen.

Passiontide

Draw closer to us with Your love, O Lord, as we enter
   into the solemnity of Your passion;
As we move into the shadowy darkness of Jerusalem –
   the city that murders its prophets;
That stones God's messengers, scourges and wounds
   them, and humiliates the Son of God.

Lord, Jesus Christ, Son of God, have mercy on us sinners
   as we contemplate our unworthiness;
Our failures and our weaknesses, stumbling and failing in
   our efforts to follow in Your steps;
Taking the arduous pathway in our feeble discipleship –
   the upward climb towards Calvary.
Cleanse our feet and every part of us;
   make us whiter than snow.
Lord, we love You with our whole heart;
   grant that we may love You always.
In Jesus, we pray.   Amen.

Maundy Thursday

Lord, kneeling in humility, we plead for cleansing, not
    only our feet but every part of us.
Draw us closer together, breaking the bread and sharing
    the cup in the timeless event of love;
Initiating for all time the most holy sacrament despite
    the presence of disloyalty and treason;
Remain with us, O Lord, as we examine ourselves and
    motives, asking, Lord is it I?

Lord, stay alongside us as we sing psalms of the
    fellowship about to crumble in disarray;
The moment of treachery and betrayal, the poisonous
    kiss, in the shadows of the olive trees;
Lord Jesus, could we not remain awake and stay beside
    You in Your time of need?
We repent of our disloyalty having pledged never to
    separate ourselves from You again.

In our vigil of sorrow, touch our hearts we pray, that we
    may strive to love You more;
And during these hours of repentance, help us make
    amends for our sinfulness;
As we stay and watch and pray and ponder our
    faithlessness in self-recrimination.
We pray these prayers in the name of Jesus, whom we
    grievously deserted. Amen.

Good Friday

O God, we behold the wondrous Cross from afar, lifted high,
   focusing our eyes in worship;
Give us courage to draw nearer, to prostrate ourselves, and
   revere the holy wood;
We linger, distressed at Your suffering, humiliation and
   anguish, weeping in the company of those whose loyalty
   and faith keeps them present to the fearful end.

May the sight of the cruel nails pierce our hearts and minds
   with deeper insights into the Pascal mystery.
In company with the centurion may we see the true reality of
   the Son of God.
The earth trembles and darkens, our dear Lord takes His last
   breath, and it is finished.
Lord Jesus Christ, Son of God, have mercy on us, sinners.   Amen.

Holy Saturday

Look down upon us, O God; why do You seem so far
    from us on this day of deep sorrow?
Why does the dark night of the soul linger on into the
    hopelessness of the daytime?
We weep, our eyes flow with tears of lamentation amid
    the heaviness of our desolation.
Christ's lifeless body left in a borrowed tomb – no place
    to lay His head in death as in life.

Have compassion upon us, O Lord God, and bring us to
    a place of new joy and consolation;
Come down, O love divine, transform our faithless
    beings and renew us with Your good news
Which banishes our sorrow and allows the true light of
    Your presence to shine upon us.
In the name of our Lord Jesus who gave himself for us
    on the Cross, we pray. Amen.

Easter

All praise and glory be to You, O Lord! Your Son Jesus
Christ is risen indeed!
Heaven and earth and all creation worship You, we raise
our voices in triumphant adulation.
The glorious company of apostles, the holy saints and
angels unite to sing Your praise;
Give us voice to join in their unending Easter Gloria to
You, our Lord and King.

For Jesus Christ has risen triumphant in glory; no longer
in the darkness of the tomb;
In the golden light of this glorious day He walks with us
and meets us by the shore;
His presence transforms the shallowness of our faith into
the vibrant Pascal joy of victory;
His robes all red from the winepress are now transfigured
into dazzling white.[1]

In the blood of the Lamb we are washed clean of our sin,
sanctified and justified
In the name of the Lord Jesus, and called into His
marvellous light.
The doors of heaven have been thrown open wide for us
to enter into the joy of the Lord.
Alleluia, Alleluia, Amen.

[1] cf. Isaiah 63:2.

Ascension

Lord Jesus Christ, ascended, crowned and glorified;
Seated at the right hand of the Father;
Away above the clouds of unknowing.
We gaze heavenwards to glimpse You.

Accessible Lord, we praise You for Your closeness;
The love that engulfs us;
The compassion that nurtures us;
The tears that You share with us;
The warmth of Your continual blessing.
We praise You in union with the Father
    and the Holy Spirit;
One God, now and always. Amen.

Pentecost

Descend upon us, O Spirit of God;
    find Your home in the depths of our being;
In our inner selves where we encounter
    the silent music of Your voice;
Your song without words which leads us into Your
    deepest mysteries;
The voice which opens our hearts to Your profound truths,
    which assure us of Your compassion and infinite love.

May Your spirit steer us away from our empty words
    that drown out Your voice,
And give us wisdom and discernment to respond
    to Your call.
May Your spirit make us a priestly people worthy
    of our calling,
And grant us our heart's desire to serve You with
    empathy and compassion.
Kindle in us the fire of Your love and raise our eyes to
    visions of Your heavenly kingdom;
Where we will be overcome by wonder,
    love and praise.   Amen.

Trinity

Creator God, source of all life, whose supreme wisdom
and power exercises dominion over all things;
Give us eyes to perceive the touch of Your creative hands
in all that is good, beautiful and delightful;
Your touch which embraces all universal life in timeless
creative growth.
May we be caught up in Your continuing act of creation,
turning our darkness into light, and transforming our
human nature through the influence of Your infinite
wisdom and integrity.

God incarnate who walked the earth, loving the despised
and the isolated, and healing the suffering;
God, falling into cruel human hands, despised, humiliated,
wounded, and left to die on Calvary's tree;
We praise You for sharing our human frailty, experiencing
fear, anxiety and despair;
You offer us an example of holy living, loving and caring
for the vulnerable and marginalized.

God, Holy Spirit, encompass us and endow us with
wisdom and understanding.
Search us out in our waywardness and discern the inner
secrets of our hearts;
Breathe upon us, speak to our hearts, enter into the depths
of our being, and transform us into Your likeness.

Triune God, Father, Son and Holy Spirit, risen, ascended
and glorified;
God above us, God beside us, God within us, we pray
You, illuminate our pathway to heaven.
Be present at our awakening, hear our dawn chorus of
praise and bring us to that place where we shall see You
in the fullness of Your glory.   Amen.

—*w*—

Saints and
Holy Days

—*w*—

St Cecilia   Patron of music and musicians   22 November

Loving God, creator of all that is good and beautiful, we give
   You thanks for Your servant Cecilia, patron saint of music
   and musicians, who, in faithful loyalty, faced martyrdom.
We thank You that You endow musicians with the creative
   powers to fashion the elements of music in a way that
   transports our spirits to heavenly realms.
We pray that all who engage in music may recognize its
   powers to touch our senses that lie beyond words and
   conceptual understanding.
We give thanks for the capacity of music to access the deepest
   crevices of our hearts and transport us to the joys of heaven.
In the name of Jesus, we pray.   Amen.

St Andrew   Apostle, Patron Saint of Ireland   30 November

Lord, our Father, we celebrate with thanksgiving the life
   of Andrew, the fisherman;
Whom Your Son recognized as a man searching for a
   true faith and purpose in life;
We give thanks that he responded to John the Baptist's
   belief in Jesus the Lamb of God;
And to his unselfish claim that Jesus was the one
   worthier of following.

Praise be to You, that Andrew heard the call of Jesus to
   come, see, and join Him.
Turning his back on home, loved ones and a life of
   fishing to attract new disciples loyal to Christ;
Bringing his brother to the Lord, and a young boy with
   his loaves to minister to the crowd;
And, as the first missionary, taking the good news to the
   farthest corners of the earth.

May we who respond to Christ's call to follow Him,
   identify with St Andrew's discipleship;
His dedication, single-minded ardour, adventurous spirit,
   and faith in facing the unknown;
And his willingness to suffer indifference, anguish and
   martyrdom in Your service, our Lord God.
In the name of Jesus, we pray.   Amen.

St John of the Cross   14 December

Lord, God, we bless You for all Your saints shining before
    us with heavenly brightness;
For St John of the Cross, mystic, theologian, poet,
    Carmelite friar and spiritual teacher;
Whose wisdom and mystical insights blessed Your Church
    with his deep holiness;
Leading us into contemplative lives in which our souls
    are infused with Your Divine Love.

May we feel Your presence as we delve into the profound
    depths of contemplation;
Celebrating St John's life, seeking Your radiant light in the
    mysterious night darkness;
Give us the courage and strength to enter with him into
    the gloom of our spiritual night,
To walk securely in Your love, still prone to doubt,
    spiritual crisis, and depression.

We praise You, Lord, that he kept the faith, despite
    betrayal, brutality and imprisonment by members of his
    own community,
Who excluded and closed their doors to him.
May we who celebrate St John of the Cross this day follow
    his example in remaining true to our trust in You,
O God, our constant companion in these times of
    deep darkness.   Amen.

St Stephen   First Martyr   26 December

O God, reassure us of Your love as the shadow of the
    Cross falls over the sleeping Christ Child;
Entering a world which He is born to save, to bring
    light and love to a people lost in darkness.
On this day when the celebration of Christmas love is
    violated by the martyrdom of St Stephen;
We thank You for this Your compassionate follower who
    did signs and wonders in Your name.

We reflect on the example of him who walked in the
    footsteps of Christ, his Lord and Master,
Facing trial before the Sanhedrin, accused of blasphemy
    because of his forthright preaching.
Lord give us grace to stand for the truth, to look
    heavenwards for Your Divine Guidance;
Inspired by Your servant Stephen, lead us from hatred to
    love, from vengeance to forgiveness.
In the power of our Lord Jesus, we pray.   Amen.

St John   **Apostle and Evangelist**   **27 December**

O God, give us Your blessing as we pay homage to Your
  loyal servant John the Evangelist;
Whose life was touched by the Divine Love of Your Son
  Jesus, his Lord, to whom he stayed close,
Experiencing wonders, miracles, joys, sadness and anguish;
  and who, during his years of reflection,
Received insights through the Spirit that teaches us
  all things.

We honour St John's life in the Spirit, stirring in him the
  deeper meaning of Christ's words.
With gratitude we contemplate his glimpses of Your
  Divine Nature, the mystery of the Word made flesh,
The love in which we are called to abide, dwelling in
  Him and He in us.
We celebrate the mystery of the Incarnation, the source
  of light and life within our souls,
By which the darkness is overcome by Your one true and
  marvellous light.
To You, Lord, be all praise and glory. Amen.

St Thomas Becket   Archbishop and Martyr   29 December

Bountiful God, we thank You for appointing prophets
and teachers to kindle our faith.
We praise You for St Thomas Becket, who, walking in
the steps of Augustine,
Strove to develop Christian life in England.
We celebrate his conversion from a lavish lifestyle as a
king's diplomat to an austere life
As a priest, archbishop and philanthropist.

O God, we praise You for his single-minded devotion to
Your church, his resilient faith in the face of
fundamental conflicts with the king whose reckless
words led to his violent assassination during his
devotions at the altar of Canterbury Cathedral.
We join our prayers with the countless pilgrims who
have travelled to his shrine, to give thanks to You, O
Lord, for this,
Your devout servant, and shepherd of souls.   Amen.

St Ælred of Rievaulx   Abbot   12 January

Praise be to You, O Lord, for all Your saints who strove to
 live in the light of Your Divine Love;
For Ælred who aspired to build a community united in
 mutual friendship and spiritual purity.
May we be inspired by his example of holy compassion,
 uniting us in the bond of peace,
And devoted to You, may we live in affection for one
 another and grow into Your likeness.

We pray that we may worship You, drawn together and
 united in spiritual affection;
In the spirit of Your love that leads us to the fulfilment of
 Your Divine Purpose in our lives;
Striving to respond to Your call to us to love one another
 as You have loved us;
That love that calls for no reward save of knowing that
 we are blessed and live in Your grace. Amen.

St Antony of Egypt   Hermit and Abbot   17 January

Lord God, we give You thanks and praise for all the
  saints who, throughout centuries past,
Have taught us how to live simple prayerful lives of self-
  control and humility.
Today we venerate Your servant Antony who
  surrendered his riches for a life of poverty, solitude
  and reflection, seeking Your companionship with
  singleness of heart and mind.

May we be inspired by his example, rejecting all that
  holds us back from lives devoted to You;
Seeking You in lives of personal discipline and prayer,
  befriending those seeking support and direction in their
  lives of prayer and contemplation,
So that at the last we may come to share the riches of
  eternal life with You and all the saints.   Amen.

Conversion of St Paul   25 January

O all-knowing and powerful Lord, God of surprises, who
    breaks through into our lives as a shining light,
A revelation of Your glory to inspire us into new realms
    of wonder and praise;
We give thanks that on the Damascus road You appeared
    before Saul as a blinding light;
Transforming him from a persecutor to Your single-
    minded and ardent apostle, Saint Paul.

Today we celebrate the wonder of his conversion,
    proclaiming him as our exemplar of a life wholly
    dedicated to You;
Sharing the good news of the Gospel to the church
    universal, filled with the fullness of Your grace and
    enriched by the baptism of the Holy Spirit.
All glory be to You O Lord, God almighty, now and
    for ever. Amen.

George Herbert   **Priest and poet**   **27 February**

We praise You, Lord, for Your powerful influence on the
    life of George Herbert;
Whom You called to priesthood in Your church, lovingly
    nurturing and caring for his flock.
Help us to share his love and richness of daily prayer
    each day of our busy lives,
Celebrating Your creative touch and presence in the
    beauty of everything around us.

We praise You for his musical gifts, and the influence of
    the Holy Spirit on his writings;
For his texts inspiring composers across the ages from
    Purcell to Vaughan Williams.
May his devotion to Your church and its people,
    reflected in his writings and ministry,
Inspire us in our Lenten journey to see You in all things
    on our way to the New Jerusalem.   Amen.

St David **Patron Saint of Wales** 1 March

Loving God, who, throughout the ages has touched the
hearts of men and women, inspiring them into lives of
devotion and sanctity.
Today we celebrate with thankful hearts the gift of David,
monk, bishop and patron saint of Wales.
We praise You for his touch and influence on the
universal church, especially in Wales and Ireland.

We give You thanks for his example of spiritual living,
holding fast to those things that are pure and eternal,
praying that, following his example, we may come to
receive with him the crown of everlasting life
with You and the Holy Spirit, ever one God, now
and always. Amen.

St Patrick   **Patron Saint of Ireland**   **17 March**

Generous God, we praise You for Your gift of St Patrick,
    patron saint of Ireland;
May we be inspired by the example of his life lived in
    humility and prayerfulness;
His firm belief and faith in Your all-embracing presence
    throughout our lives;
And in Your constant presence within and around us to
    guide and direct us into ways of holiness.

We give You praise for his obedience to Your call to live
    a life wholly in Your service;
His visionary zeal in living a contemplative life focused
    on Your Divine Guidance.
May we, inspired and energized by the example of his
    profound dedication to You,
Come to dwell with him in Your everlasting joy with all
    the saints and angels of heaven.   Amen.

St Joseph of Nazareth

God our Father, we praise You for Joseph of Nazareth and
his role in the gospel story;
For his integrity, loyalty to the Virgin Mary and his
attentiveness to the messages of the angels;
His obedience to Your call to take Mary as his wife,
nurturing and loving Your Son as his own;
Sharing with Jesus his carpentry skills with rough wood,
foreshadowing the wood and nails of the Cross.

O God, may we be inspired by his example of alertness to
the movements of the Spirit;
To share with him the gifts of humility, compassion and
obedience to Your holy will;
Assist us in protecting the vulnerable and the abandoned as
we walk in the steps of our Lord Jesus Christ, through
whom we pray. Amen.

St George   Martyr, Patron Saint of England   23 April

Lord God, we thank and praise You for valiant St George,
  patron saint of England and martyr,
Whose life of good deeds and valour are known
  only to You.
We pray for all those threatened by unseen and
  destructive forces, both real and imaginary;
Give them confidence in Your unfailing love and
  protection in their hours of darkness.

Hear our prayers for all those who work for peace and
  harmony and strive for justice;
Giving thanks in their efforts to maintain human rights,
  equality and dignity.
On this day when we observe the festival of St George and
  honour his memory,
May we come to rejoice with him in the triumph of
  Your glorious Resurrection;
Through Jesus Christ our Lord.   Amen.

St Mark   **Evangelist**   **25 April**

Praise be to You, O God, for St Mark, eyewitness of the
earthly ministry of Jesus Your Son;
For his steadfast faith and foresight in his authorship of
the first Gospel narrative;
For the immediacy and urgency of his testimony of new
life in Christ that influenced and inspired other
Evangelists to affirm the life-changing Gospel message.

We give thanks for his role in supporting the missionary
work of the early church;
For his companionship and loyalty to Saints Paul, Peter
and Barnabas in their work of proclaiming the gospel
throughout the wider world,
Whereby we might all believe that Jesus Christ is Lord, our
strength and our song, through whom we pray. Amen.

Julian of Norwich   Spiritual writer and mystic   8 May

O God we hold before You those who live in prayerful
    solitude in communion with Jesus Christ;
Praising You for Julian of Norwich who sought to
    comprehend the mystery of Divine Love;
Seeking in her interior silence life-changing and deeper
    insights into the holy incarnation;
And through Your grace receiving awesome and
    inexpressible revelations.

May we, like her, be inspired to identify with Christ by
    walking the way of the Cross;
Developing deeper insights into His pain and suffering
    that revealed the fullness of His love;
Binding us together in His passion to live in holiness
    and righteousness all our days;
And to rise with Him on the last day to the unspeakable
    joys of the heavenly places.
Through Jesus Christ our Lord.   Amen.

St Matthias   Apostle   14 May

Father, we thank You that by the power of the Spirit
    Matthias was chosen to be an apostle;
A worthy disciple of Your Son throughout his
    ministry, becoming one of the twelve after the death
    of a betrayer;
A witness to His baptism, His teaching and acts of
    healing, His Resurrection and ascension.

Help us discern the movements of the Spirit in our lives
    and empower us by Your love.
May we follow in the wake of St Matthias and become
    faithful and upright servants;
Proclaiming the Good News to the world and giving our
    lives unreservedly in Your service.
Through Jesus, our Lord and Master, we pray. Amen.

St Barnabas   Apostle   11 **June**

Lord, our Father, we praise You that You called St Barnabas to
    be an apostle;
A man of faith who discerned Your call to serve You and
    walk in the footsteps of Your Son;
Giving all that he possessed to the church and offering
    support to St Paul from the beginning;
Recognizing in him his ardour and zeal to establish and
    nurture the early church.

We praise You for his commitment in faithfully supporting
    St Paul's mission to the Gentiles;
And accompanying him on his journeys to spread the good
    news of the Gospel of Christ.
May we, in following his example, devote ourselves in life-
    long service, faithfully serving You to the end of our days.
We offer this prayer in the name of our Lord, Jesus Christ. Amen.

St Peter and St Paul   Apostles   29 June

Praise be to You, O Lord, for the touch of the Holy Spirit
    on the lives of St Peter and St Paul;
For their influence on the spiritual life of the universal
    church throughout the ages.
We give thanks to You, O Lord, for St Peter, the rock,
    entrusted with the keys of heaven;
Capable of great insight, loyalty and love for You.

We praise You for St Paul's powerful conversion, his
    rabbinic grasp of the Hebrew Scriptures,
His single-minded mission to the Gentile church, and to
    reconcile theological differences.
May we, inspired by the influence of the Holy Spirit
    uniting them in life and in death,
Build Your church in ecumenical understanding, serving
    You faithfully all our days,
O Lord, our strength and our song, now and always.   Amen.

St Thomas   Apostle   3 July

O God, we bless and praise You for St Thomas, Your gift to all
who seek a sure faith;
Risen Lord, reveal yourself to us who seek the reassurance of
Your comforting presence.
We bring before You in prayer those who experience
uncertainty and times of doubt;
Draw close with Your reassuring touch and strengthen our
faith when it wavers.

We give thanks for St Thomas's discernment in declaring
Jesus as his Lord and his God;
Proclaiming His divinity and prompting Jesus's explanation
that he is the Way, the Truth and the Life.
May we, like St Thomas, be prepared to give our lives
in Your service;
And to spread the Gospel of Christ to the whole world.
Through Christ Jesus, we pray. Amen.

St Mary Magdalene   22 July

Praise to You, Lord, for the inspiration of
  Mary Magdalene, Your penitent and loyal follower.
Let us see in her deep devotion and gratitude the wonder
  of Your generous and healing love.
Seeing her profound penitence may we, in humility, fall at
  Your feet and wash them in our tears.
As we ponder her act of extravagant love, give us grace to
  be inspired and devoted wholly to You;
The grace to contemplate the extent of her deep
  devotion to You, her Lord and Saviour.

We give You praise for her ardent ministry to Him in life,
  leading her to the side of the Cross, and the graveside;
Mary of Magdala, who went out weeping and returned
  with shouts of joy;
The Apostle to the Apostles proclaiming to the world the
  good news of the Gospel of our Lord Jesus, through
  whom, and in whom we pray.   Amen.

Mary, Martha and Lazarus of Bethany 29 July

Lord, we give You thanks for the example of Mary,
  Martha, and Lazarus;
For welcoming You, our Lord, into their Bethany home;
For while the birds had nests and foxes their holes,
  the Son of Man had nowhere to lay His head,
Until finding in Bethany a refuge, hospitality and communion.

We praise You for Martha who offered Him her attentive
  and fervent care;
For Mary who reached out with empathy; and Lazarus
  whom Jesus loved.
Lord of the homeless, may You find this openness of
  welcome through the doors of our hearts,
And give us grace to receive You and allow you to take
  possession of our souls.

Give us grace that we may offer generous hospitality to
  You, our God, like theirs.
May we welcome You into the dwelling place of our
  inner beings, Father, Son and Holy Spirit;
To whom, through whom, and in whom we pray.   Amen.

Hail! Blessed Virgin, mother of our Lord Jesus Christ,
   God incarnate.
May we, inspired by her courage, purity and devotion,
Join her in praising the name of the Lord in her joyful
   song of salvation.

Praise God, whose Spirit, falling afresh on her, made a
   dwelling place for the Holy Child in her womb;
Who, with love and deep devotion nurtured the Christ
   Child, the light of the world, at her breast;
Caressing the defenceless naked babe close to the heart
   that in time would be pierced,[2]
As she with tender love and grief gently laid Him to rest
   in the silent and lonely tomb;

Now, rejoicing with her in the good news that the Lord
   has risen indeed, and following her example;
May we walk in His steps and serve our risen and
   ascended Lord with love and devotion all our days.
Let us praise the blessed Virgin Mary who found a place
   in her womb for our Lord Jesus;
And may we, likewise, be inspired to make room in our
   hearts for God, with us today and always.   Amen.

[2] cf. Luke 2:33.

St Bartholomew   Apostle   24 August

Praise be to You, O Lord, that You search us out and
    know us from the very core of our being;
Viewing us from afar and calling us as You called
    trustworthy Bartholomew.
You sought him out to follow You in a life dedicated to
    preach Your message:
Today, we commemorate him and his moment of
    revelation, recognizing You as the Son of God.

May we, similarly fired with the gifts of the Spirit, and
    inspired by the good news of the Resurrection,
Praise You for his work in spreading the gospel widely
    through foreign parts of the world.
Glory be to You, O God, for the example of Your true
    and loyal Apostle, Bartholomew;
Who, strong, ardent and courageous in the faith,
    went to his painful death of martyrdom,
    upheld by great visions of angels.[3]
Raise us up, O Lord, that we may ever be fired by Your
    love, and praise Your name, now and for ever.   Amen.

[3] cf. John 1:50–1. Barnabas and Nathaniel are often thought to have been the same person.

Holy Cross   14 September

In the name of God, Father, Son and Holy Spirit;
We gaze in anguish on the solitary crosses high up on the
  abandoned hillside of Golgotha;
Aware of our capacity for mockery; for repentance; and to
  hear Christ's promise of life eternal,
We contemplate the Cross, the instrument of death, on
  which hung the Prince of Life;
Lifted high above us, revealing the mystic glow of the
  place where the world is redeemed.

Lord, give us grace and courage to approach Calvary's
  tree, trembling to touch its holy wood.
May the symbol of love outpoured ever linger on in our
  minds, in body, soul and gesture;
Giving us strength to face suffering in the company of
  Him who suffered for our sake;

Whose outstretched arms bring us healing and teach us
  to live in obedience and humility;
Fill us, heart and soul, with the fire of Your love,
  banishing the lingering darkness within;
To illuminate our pathway by Your saving grace, singing
  the mighty song of our redemption;
And confessing that Jesus Christ is Lord;
  to the glory of God the Father.   Amen.

St Hildegard of Bingen   Benedictine abbess   17 September

Lord God, we give You thanks for the life and inspiration
    of Your servant, Hildegard;
Whom You blessed with visionary, poetic and musical insights,
Opening up for her a new world of theological,
    liturgical and artistic life,
All dedicated to her love for You and to glorify You, her
    Lord and Master.
We are thankful that she became more than the mere
    totality of these qualities,
And praise You for the symphony of gifts made manifest
    within her creative mind;
May her legacy inspire us, Lord, to bring integration to
    our fragmented lives;
Teaching us to sing a new song and to approach the
    mystery of things untouchable and unseen;

May she inspire us to love all living things and to
    challenge injustice and corruption in the world;
And create a vision within us of light, beauty and
    splendour in Your holy sanctuary.
We give thanks for Hildegard, a lantern burning to
    illuminate the sacramental life of Your church;
Taking us to the very threshold of heaven to glory in the
    harmonic song of the angels and the saints.
May we, with her, continue to make music to You, our
    Lord God, as long as we have our being.   Amen.

St Matthew Apostle and Evangelist 21 September

We thank You, Lord, for Your friendship of the outcast
  and compassion to the despised,
And for calling Matthew to leave the seat of custom and
  follow You as Lord and Saviour;
Leaving behind his life of tax-collecting and the
  contempt of his fellow Jews,
To devote himself to Jesus in whose company he was
  transformed and given new life,
And shared a life of healing and teaching, and seeing
  miracles of lives being changed.

We praise You, God, that he perceived the prophetic
  thread of Your ultimate purposes;
Recognizing Jesus as the heir of David and the fulfilment
  of Your plan for humankind.
We praise You for St Matthew's literary skill, declaring
  Jesus as the Saviour of the World,
And, hearing Your call to spread the gospel, proclaiming
  the Christian message across the whole world. Amen.

St Michael and All Angels   29 September

Holy and gracious God, be with us in our fearfulness
   and keep us safe in Your love;
May St Michael and all the holy angels protect us from
   anxiety and harmful attacks.
We pray that he, the herald of heaven and helper of the
   helpless, protect us from all evil.
Lord, may Your holy angels watch over those crushed in
   spirit and dispel their darkness;
Set Your love upon us and comfort us with the radiance
   of Your continual blessing.

Most holy God, we raise our eyes in wonder at the
   celestial brightness of Your kingdom;
And, at the end of our earthly pilgrimage when we
   hear the trumpet call of judgement day,
May St Michael and all the angels of the
   heavenly host,
Be with us in wonder, love and praise in the singing
   of our final Sanctus at the end of time.
Praise and honour and glory be to Him who sits on
   the throne, and to the Lamb for ever.   Amen.

St Francis of Assisi   4 October

Glory and praise to You, O gracious God, for revealing
   yourself in the wonders of the universe;
And for Francis, Your servant, who cherished all Your
   creations as his brothers and sisters;
Who found great joy and delight in the inherent
   goodness and beauty of Your world;
The richness of the harvest of the earth and the rhythm
   of the seasons.
May we, meditating before Your holy Cross, hear Your still
   small voice, and, in response,
Re-build Your universal Church into one of compassion,
   love, unity and understanding.

We praise You, Lord, for the life and example of Your
   fervent companion, Francis.
May we, following in his footsteps and attempting to find
   our vocation in lives of self-denial,
Humility, generosity and contemplation, draw near to
   Your call to a simple way of life,
That leads us ever towards lives dedicated
   wholly to You.
In the name of Jesus, we pray.   Amen.

St Teresa of Avila   15 October

Praise to You, Lord God, for the inspiration and
    enlightenment of the Holy Spirit;
Illuminating our pathway to the unseen realities of Your
    Divine Nature.
We give thanks to You, O God, for the life and example of
    Teresa of Avila,
To whom You revealed yourself with powerful mystical
    visions of Your holy presence in her life.

Like her, may we enter into that sanctuary of Your
    dwelling place at the centre of our being,
And, transforming our ways into Your ways and all our
    thoughts into contemplation,
Surrender fully to You and, developing that intimacy
    with Your Divine Presence,
And discarding the robes of ego and all trivial
    attachments, find the place of consolation.

Lord, in times of anxiety and distress, cherish us with
    visions of eternity
And, responding to the mystery of Your love, may we
    learn to live in awe of Your presence,
Finding that spiritual pathway which leads ever onward
    to the ecstasy of Your eternal glory.   Amen.

God of truth and love, we give You thanks for the gift of
St Luke, Evangelist and physician;
Who, in his colourful writing highlighted the words and
wonders of Your Son Jesus Christ,
As he walked the earth among us, engaging with the
marginalized and outcasts of society,
Luke sharing His concern for the plight of women, the
poor, and needy.

Praise to You, Lord, for Luke who, like us, did not
encounter Jesus in the flesh,
Yet closely identified with Him and, seeing His
compassion for the sick and the suffering,
Resonated with the wonder and mystery of His Master's
miraculous healing powers,
Which flowed from the energy emanating from prayer
and contemplation with You, his Father.

Lord, we celebrate his loyalty to Paul, companion in
mission and times of imprisonment.
Different in temperament and tradition, together they
spoke universal truths of our faith,
United in their love for You, and taking the news of
salvation to the world's ends.
To You, our Father in heaven, be all praise and glory. Amen.

All Saints

Almighty God we proclaim Your great and glorious name;
And sing our praise and gratitude for the lives and living
    example of all Your saints;
Witnesses and martyrs of the faith who have come
    through the great ordeal;
And who worship You day and night within Your temple.

We thank You for the teaching and example of those who
    have stood valiantly, steadfast to Your name;
Shining forth as beacons of faith and love, and leading us
    into a living faith.
Lord, give us grace to follow in the footsteps of the
    glorious company of all the saints;
And, united with them with joy in our hearts, worship
    You in songs of everlasting praise.

May we, gathered around the altar of sacrifice and love
    here on earth, be ever drawn
Into communion together with the great celestial
    company of angels and saints;
To stand with the great multitude that no one can count
    before the throne of the Lamb;
Blessing and honour and glory and power be yours
    for ever and ever.　Amen.

All Souls   2 November

Lord, we come in thanksgiving, remembering those for
    whom we have cared and loved;
Those You have called by name and who have left our
    uncertain world of distress and tears;
We bring to You those who continue to abide in our
    hearts and in our memories.
Hear us as we name them before You in our silent prayers.

Pause to remember or name those who have died.

We praise You that they have ascended to Your glory
    with our love in their hearts;
That they have seen the holy city, the new Jerusalem,
    and now abide in Your kingdom.

On that day when we are called to that heavenly place
    where grief and crying are no more,
We pray that we shall rise in peace and tranquillity, to
    see Your table spread before us,
And be received in glory, our heads anointed with oil
    and wearing the crown of everlasting life;
Where everything is made new in the company of the
    angels and all the saints;
With You, our God and King, to whom be glory and
    honour for ever and ever.   Amen.

Special Prayers

Baptism and Confirmation

Lord, our Father, we bring before You in prayer all those
engaged in a journey of faith.
Give them enquiring hearts and minds which lead to a
deeper faith and confidence in Your love.
In their formation give them new levels of commitment
to live according to Your guidance.
We pray for their teachers as they nurture and inspire
them in their desire to know You more deeply each
day of their lives.
Through Jesus Christ our Lord.   Amen.

Spiritual well-being

Wait upon the Lord in stillness, O my soul,
To hear the music of His still, small voice;
Tune my heart to the healing touch of His Divine Presence;
May every breath I take give voice to sing of His glory.

Search me out and know me, O Lord, know my heart
and examine every thought.
Teach me Your ways and lead me in the paths of peace;
And prepare me to enter into Your heavenly courts with
joy and delight.
In the name of Jesus, I pray.   Amen.

Devotion

God of beauty, wisdom, truth and light,
   dwell with us with visions of holiness;
God of compassion,
   create in us loving and merciful hearts;
God of forgiveness,
   heal us of our heartless grievances.
God of comfort and joy,
   may we praise You with all our being;
Give us wings to fly to new heights of delight
   in Your heavenly kingdom;
And transport us to that celestial place of great joy
   in the company of the angels.   Amen.

Counsellors and befrienders

Lord, our loving Father, we thank You for listening to the
   cries of those in distress;
Comforter of the anxious and sorrowful, we pray for all
   who need help and understanding.
We give thanks for the gifts of those whom You call to
   work as counsellors and befrienders;
Who lay aside their own concerns and anxieties to hear
   the problems and pain of others.

Lord God, just as Jesus encountered the woman at the
   well with empathy and insight;
May counsellors perceive their clients' deeper needs
   whilst acknowledging those they present.
Inspire them with Your gift of compassion, to respond
   with sensitivity and kindness,
To demonstrate the full extent of the love that took Your
   Son all the way to the Cross.
Glory be to Jesus, through whom we pray.   Amen.

The depressed and the suicidal

Draw near, O Lord, to those brought low in deep sadness;
    raise them up in hope.
For those who feel cast adrift, lonely and unloved;
    be their constant companion.
Lord, sufferer of pain, bereavement and loss;
    have compassion for those who grieve;
Be with those who find themselves shrouded in dark
    clouds of sorrow; bring them comfort.
Show Your empathy to those in desolation;
    bring them to a time of consolation.
Stay with those who weep alongside a dying friend;
    may they feel Your compassion.
Dispel the dry bones of old memories, wounds and hurts;
    replace them with forgiveness.
Draw near to those who have no hopes of a future;
    deliver them from closed and locked doors.
Save the vulnerable from their enemies and their demons,
    from feelings of isolation and desperation;
Be alongside those in despair at the edge of the precipice;
    draw them back from the brink.
Save those who have no one to pull them back and to
    cling to them at their time of need.
Ever loving God, our Saviour and our Redeemer. Amen.

Climate change

Lord, our creator God, who fashioned the world to be good
and beautiful;
May we continue to live and praise Your name for Your
Divine Touch on all that surrounds us.
Help us to be continually mindful to conserve all the
richness of Your creation;
The land, sea and air which, through our folly and selfish
ways, are in danger of pollution.

We earnestly pray for peoples in those parts of the world
who experience at first hand the effects of global warming:
flood, drought, famine, disease, starvation and death.
We do earnestly repent of our sinful and mindless extravagance.
Forgive our ignorance and deafness to Your call to amend our
ways, and give us a new vision
To see the fragile beauty of all that You have placed into
our hands.
Lord, hear us, graciously hear us, in the name of Christ. Amen.

World peace

Almighty God, our heavenly Father, we pray for the
world that You created in which we might live in peace
and harmony.
We pray that leaders of all nations may govern in the way
of equity and righteousness, renouncing all
manifestations of injustice and corruption.
Through Your Divine Influence move repressive regimes to
adopt more democratic structures so that Your kingdom
of peace may reign on earth as it does in heaven.
Through Jesus Christ our Lord. Amen.

The lonely and the unloved

Lord of the lonely and the unloved
   draw near, touch and embrace them;
Lord, of the abandoned and the neglected
   come and give them comfort;
Lord of those in danger
   keep watch and protect them;
Lord of the anxious and fearful
   give Your reassurance and security;
Lord of the weeping and distressed
   dry their tears and gently hold them;
Lord of the suffering
   show Your compassion and steadfast love;
Lord of the dying
   be close, and give them visions of Your eternal home;
In the name of our Lord Jesus, we pray.   Amen.

Healing

Lord, our loving Father, as the day draws to a close,
Help us to leave behind all the turbulence and turmoil
   of the day;
Come to us in stillness as we reflect on our need for
   Your closeness,
For Your healing touch on every aspect of our lives.
May we draw You into the recesses of our minds,
Where hover our feelings of frailty, vulnerability and anxiety;
Our awareness of the depths of our fear and awareness of
   our deepest needs.

Lord of compassion and mercy, draw near, placing Your
   healing hands upon us
With Your sense of peace and wholeness.
In the name of our Saviour, Jesus Christ.   Amen.

The sick and the needy

Hear us, O Lord, as we pray for all those who are
suffering ill health and mental distress;
Especially for those who are struggling to come to terms
with a terminal illness.
Bring them relief in their anguish and reassure them of
Your constant presence and endless love.
We pray for all their doctors, nurses and care workers that
they may receive sufficient strength and resilience in all
their duties.
May they recognize Your Divine Presence in their daily
commitment to support those placed within their care.
In the name of Jesus, we pray. Amen.

The National Health Service

Loving and caring God, we thank You for calling women
and men to the ministry of healing;
For those working in hospitals as doctors, nurses, support
workers and chaplains.
May they be aware of and responsive to Your guidance as
they perform their duties of care,
Restoring patients to health and wellbeing with
attentiveness, empathy and altruism.

Look upon them with compassion as they struggle in
times of stress and unrelenting pressure.
Give them wisdom, resilience, and reassurance as they
accompany those on the edge of life;
May those breathing their last in fear, anguish and
isolation be reassured by the security of Your love
and generosity, manifest in the dedication of Your
servants here on earth.
Lord God, we pray in the name of Jesus, our healer. Amen.

Church music and musicians

Praise to You, Lord, that You have created in us the desire
  for music;
Music that lifts to new heights the imagination of our souls.
Keep us, Your servants of music, from any display of pride
  that obscures Your presence;
Your Divine Presence which renders us receptive to the
  harmony of Your grace.
Open our ears to draw us into the miracle of Your created
  soundscape of beauty;
Music that lifts us to the holy mountain, bringing us face to
  face with You, our transfigured Lord.

Praise to You, Lord, for the music that opens the gateway to
  the depths of our hearts;
The things untaught, yet sensed through the influence of
  the Holy Spirit;
The world of the Spirit which we cannot articulate beyond
  the language of music;
That universal language of Pentecost accessible to all peoples;
That lends us access to the deeper crevices of our inner lives.

May our valiant efforts to worship You through music rise
  before You, O Lord;
Modulating to new heights of celestial harmony, resounding
  for all eternity in heavenly places;
May we come to Your eternal kingdom, that world without
  end where, at the gate, we are welcomed with the
  celestial trumpets that sound for us on the other side.
Where we come face to face with St Cecilia and all the
  saints, angels and archangels;
In concert with the angelic choirs singing our eternal
  Sanctus before Your heavenly throne.   Amen.

The marginalized

Lord, we pray for those who are marginalized in our society;
For all Your children, regardless of age, colour, creed, sexuality
and life style;
We repent of our discriminatory attitudes towards those
deemed to be different;
Repenting of our judgemental stance towards those we
perceive as deviant;
Those driven by our hostility to the fringes of society;
Those who struggle with the resultant lack of identity;
Burdened with feelings of unworthiness and low self-esteem.

We pray for those who feel unworthy to come under the roof
of the Church;
And repent of our Pharisaic stance towards the stranger.
We pray with sorrow for those who feel abandoned by
Your church;
Those who feel unwelcome and banished from its doors;

Convict us, O Lord, for our silent complicity in the
harassment of the ostracized;
Complicit by our silence and lack of support
for the isolated;
Forgive us as we pass by on the other side;
Where You, Lord Jesus, are to be found ministering and
binding up the wounds of our victims.
Show us, good Lord, how to open our arms wide to love
those whom the world despises.
Lord, whose love for all Your people took You to the Cross;
Help us to live out our calling to love them all
as You love us.   Amen.

Vocation

Lord, our Father, stay close to us in the silent hours
of the night;
In the stillness of the small hours may we become
fully aware of Your presence;
Recognizing Your gentle voice amid the clamour
of our overcrowded minds.
May we be receptive to Your voice in those
moments when You search us out;
Calling us by name and hearing Your words,
'You are mine'.[4]

Give us the resolve to respond to Your words
'follow me' and 'come and see';
Give us grace to discern Your hopes for us, and
quieten our own ambitions and desires;
Give us the courage to look into Your face and
utter those words: 'Here am I, send me forth;
Lord, take my life, and let it be dedicated to You.'

We present ourselves to You, Lord, offering nothing
more than the life You first gave us.
May we feel Your hands of blessing upon us as You
send us out into the world;
To reshape it by living out Your love, healing the
sick, the deaf and blind and resisting injustice.
May attentiveness to the movements of the Holy
Spirit be our constant rule of life;
Trusting with all our heart, and heeding Your
words to be not wise in our own sight;
And in this way, perpetually walk in the steps of
Jesus our Lord, through whom we pray.   Amen.

[4] cf. Isaiah 43:1.

Nations of the world

Lord, our Father, we pray for the world which You
created to be beautiful and peaceful;
A world which reflects the touch of Your creative hands
and Your abundant love.
How long, O Lord, will the nations tear it apart, causing
turmoil and violating human rights?
How long will violent dictatorships imprison dissidents
who protest against corruption?

We pray for those countries where political and
economic ideologies come into conflict;
And that polarized positions be resolved democratically
to establish justice, peace and harmony.
Lord God, we pray that the good news of Your love may
be proclaimed to all the world,
So that all the peoples may praise You and the earth bring
forth its increase.
These things we pray through Jesus, the Saviour of the
world. Amen.

For seafarers

We pray for all those who go down to the sea in ships;
For those who fish in deep waters and face harsh and
dangerous conditions.
Protect, we pray, all sailors and seafarers and those who
risk their lives at sea.
O Lord, who stills stormy waves, keep watch over them,
and bring them to calm waters.
In Christ's name, we pray. Amen

SLG PRESS PUBLICATIONS

slgpress.co.uk